Lauren Yoder

As someone in long-term recovery, I was not sure what to expect upon reading 100 Days (sober). Would it be one big war story, or would it contain a bunch of feel good fluff that had nothing substantial? I was pleased it contained neither. Instead, author Lauren shares a little about her past trouble and a lot about her present successes.

I enjoyed the conversational tone it was written in as well as the quotes. I found these entries to be inspiring, as there were lessons she shared I could apply to my own life.

If you have never battled an addiction, reading this gives you an opportunity to experience firsthand what those who fight this battle go through not only during, but long after they get sober.

If you are currently struggling with substance abuse/drinking this book is great. Lauren shares her victories and successes with you. She gives reason to chase after sobriety. For someone who is currently starting their walk into recovery, they will gain hope life continues to get better. In 100 Days, Lauren lets us know that there is a better life in recovery!

-David Stoecker, LCSW, MRSS-P, Director of Better Life in Recovery

Lauren Yoder

100 Days

(sober)

by

Lauren Yoder

Cover Design by Randy Craig

Lauren Yoder

IBSN-13: 978-1514398708
ISBN-10: 1514398702

Printed in the U.S.A.

To my parents

Mark and Linda

Who loved me, even when
I didn't love myself

Lauren Yoder

Contents

100 Days (sober)

Foreword

Lauren invites readers to sit down at her table where she dishes out big servings of love, washed down with miraculous 'wine turned into water' of forgiveness. Lastly, she rolls out beauteous gratitude for dessert. In this reader's estimation, she illustrated the idea that 'In God's Economy, nothing is wasted.'

Lauren pens her innermost experiences in recovery in the hopes of making her life count in your life, and I think she was successful.

As I turned the pages of her book, I found myself immersed in her healing journey, and became grateful to her parents, friends, and supports as if they were my own support network. Indeed, she has illustrated her "100 Days" as a living witness that there is transmutation and triumph after heartbreak.

Her book might help unbreak a reader's heart with its healing balm.

–Timothy Cameron AKA 'The Incomplete Skeptic', Public Speaker, Writer

Foreword 2

It has been quite a journey; or should I say rollercoaster ride with our dear daughter. I am so very thankful that she is finally nurturing her family and loving life as she was meant to. Her father and I have never stopped loving her or stopped praying for her.

In the beginning of the book Lauren refers to different situations. These are from her perspective; I could write a book from my perspective! But this is HER STORY and how she saw them.

I have really enjoyed hearing her heart and learn some of her thoughts as she was down in the valley, but now she is climbing up the mountain, and we are very thankful for her determination and tenacity through this very difficult time in her life.

Blessed to be Lauren's mom

–Linda DeJarnatt

Preface

My name is Lauren, and I'm a grateful, recovering alcoholic/addict. This book is a collection of my thoughts and advice I wish I could have given myself 20 years ago. It is 100 days of journal entries; 100 days in my sobriety. These are not the first 100 days. The Lord knows I wasn't coherent enough to think straight, none the less write. After about 7 months of sobriety, I started a blog. I started keeping a journal of my ideas, of how I thought and felt; how I was compared to how I am now. This is my second book. My previous book, *From the Weeds*, is a collection of poems from all stages of my life: from depression and addiction to recovery and hope.

These are just my thoughts based on my life experiences. I started out by finding a quote or saying and writing my feelings about it. It is interesting to see how my thinking changes the longer I am sober. How it did change and still is on a daily basis.

Introduction

I grew up in a Christian home, went to a Christian school, and was a good kid. After 6th grade, I started going to a public school. I'm not saying that because that's what got me into drugs and alcohol at all. I was very involved in sports and was really good in the high hurdles in track. I could have gone to college on a scholarship but threw that out the window when I took senior skip day and went to a big party, so missed track practice that night. Our coach had told us if we missed that practice we would be kicked off the track team. So needless to say I no longer had a chance to go to college on a scholarship. Anyways, that was just the beginning of the chain of bad decisions I started making.

I still ended up going to college. I went to a local community college, Illinois Central College to get an Associate degree, then I went off to another local college for my Bachelor of Business Administration degree.

So back in high school, I got into drugs and alcohol. I'm not going to get specific because I don't need to romanticize about it. Anyways, I continued this for some years. Then I met an amazing man, got married and had 2 beautiful children. I didn't use drugs or drink when I was pregnant with them, but after breastfeeding I would start drinking again. Drugs weren't so much a problem after we had kids, but I could never stop drinking for good. 'It is legal you know', so that was my excuse. I don't know how I stopped using while I was pregnant, but I guess it wasn't about me anymore, it was all about them, and giving them a safe environment to live in. Shortly after our second child I started drinking again, heavily. I pretty much isolated myself from everyone: all my friends, family, everyone. I didn't want anyone to know, but I was always sick, sick when I drank, sick when I didn't. I missed family functions, a lot of important things a mom should not miss. But I am not going to talk about all the bad things.

I have changed my life for the better now and will elaborate on that!!! I pretty much had an intervention from my husband and parents. They told me to go to treatment or they were done. They had tried so many times to help me, but I first had to help myself. So they called a drug/alcohol hotline February 9th, 2014 at 10:40 pm. I told them I had to go away. I would not stay local. I needed to go away, far away, to find me. So they talked for a while on the phone to the representative and shortly after, they had a flight booked for me the next day to go to Palm Springs, California at

6:40 am. And that is just the beginning.

So I'm getting ready to go to treatment. I leave Illinois with the temp of 17 deg. and land in California with a temp of 84. Wow, what a difference! So I get there, and detox for 10 days. They said it was the worst detox they had seen and I was almost taken to the hospital a few times. When I finally became coherent, or what I thought was coherent (They aren't lying when they say your head won't be clear for the first 30 days.) I was ready to get better. At first, I was just going to please everyone. I figured if I went to treatment, they would "heal" me and I would be able to "drink like others." NOT TRUE. I will never be able to drink again. I will die. I won't ever be able to "just have one drink." Because it wouldn't be just one drink, probably not even one bottle.

Once I started listening and learning about all the physical, emotional, and psychological damage, I really started paying attention. I learned more about myself in those 45 days than I probably ever had. I really started thinking about all the damage I had done, not only to my body, and my brain, but all those who I loved, all those who loved me more than I could love myself. I had to learn to love me. I had to learn how to FEEL again. Wow, was that hard! Not really FEELING for years brings a lot to the surface. I had 15 different feelings, pulling me 15 different ways. I was happy and sad and mad and grateful and sorry and blessed ALL at the same time. My head was spinning. As my roommate there said, "it was the tornado effect." (Thanks Nina!)

I started writing a blog at 7 months sober. This book is an edited version of those entries. They are titled as '100 days', not at how many days sober I was at the time. I hope you enjoy!

Day 1

I was in California, waking up every morning at 5:00 am to drink my green tea and watch the sun rise with my buddy, Cody. Every morning, I would ramble on about something and he would just sit there in "his" chair, sweatpants and hoodie on, and listen to me. Nina would listen to me until midnight, sobbing. Shane & Alex would play guitar and sing. Those people became family. I would spend all day, every day with them. We talked about some stuff that I wouldn't talk to family about. It is easier to talk to someone who is or has been in the same boat as me then a good friend who hasn't been. We all had something take over and ruin our lives. We all needed help, and were getting better together. When I first got there I figured, I would meet people, learn some stuff, get better, go home and get on with my life. But in reality I got there, met some great people, learned a lot about myself, and still stay in contact with most of the people I was there with. We are still there for each other today. There to reach out to, anytime, when a craving hits, lonely, or just to talk. When I got sober, I thought I would lose friends, but that's when I found who my real friends were. I DO just want to say, I do not have anything against alcohol or those who can drink "normally". I just can't drink. I AM STILL FUN BEING SOBER!!! Some people think that when you get sober, your life is boring. NO!!! This is when I get to enjoy life now, and not waste it, being miserable. I have learned not to take anything for granted.

Day 2

Today, I am going to share story of my car accident that was the wake up call to me getting sober.

January 28, 2014 5:23am

I wake up, and look up and see 3219. I stop and think. What just happened? Those are house numbers. Why am I laying sideways? in my car? in the snow? My legs are scrunched up tight. I can't move. I'm freaking out. "Get me out of here!!!" I scream. "Get me outta here!!!" I see the lights flashing behind me. The paramedics must already be here. How long was I out? How did I get here? I think for a minute. I was on my way to work. I remember leaving the gas station, and turning right...and that was it. I hear a man behind me breaking out the rear drivers' side window. He tells me they are working on getting me out. I ask him what happened. He said I was driving down the road and went off the road, through a few yards, flipped my car on its side, and ran into a house. What???" It was 15 houses down from the gas station. Did I black out? Did I hit ice? I don't remember. There was a big rock in front of the house that stopped me from going further into the house. So I lay there...stuck...I can't move my legs...freaking out. "Get me outta here!!!" The fireman is reaching in the car, from the back window, to hold my hand, to comfort me. Still I scream. I just want out! He gives me his coat to cover my body. They are going to break out the rear windshield to get me out. The glass shatters. I'm not usually claustrophobic, but I can't move my legs. I feel trapped. I just want out. I just want to run. I just want to go home. The fireman tells me, they are working as fast as they can to safely get me out. I sit there and think, how bad am I hurt? My legs aren't broken, just trapped. My foot hurts, but probably just cut and bruised. My left arm hurts, but just bruised. My neck is burned from the seatbelt. I can move everything, so I'm just beat up a little. I scream again. "Get me outta here! Get me outta here!!!" I must have yelled that 100 times. It seems like I have been in here for hours. I had no concept of time. I wonder how long it has been stuck here? It is so cold. I remember the weatherman saying "high of 31 degrees today, with a wind-chill of 17" and is only like 5 something in the am. I am freezing. The fireman continues to hold my hand as I scream. He then tells me they are going to have to saw the roof of my car to get me out. "What??? Not my car? You can't do that!! Just get me out!!! I'm fine. Just let me climb out!" He tells me to cover my head and body completely with his coat, to protect me. It's so dark, so loud. I hear the chainsaw start up. It cuts through the metal and I feel the vibrations all through my body. It seems like forever. It is so loud...and close to my head. I just keep screaming. "Get me out!!!!!" 43 minutes later I am extracted from my car. I am put onto a flat board carefully and into the ambulance. And the rest is another story.

Day 3

I'm not quite ready for fall yet. I'm supposed to do a couple things with the family today outside. Brrrr! Tomorrow I am doing a walk for Juvenile Diabetes. My nephew and a couple nieces have diabetes. Last year this time, I would have been too selfish to do anything to help anyone out. But it's not all about me anymore, so I'm doing what I can to help someone else out. I've learned not to take anything or anyone for granted. You never know what can happen.

In one of my readings this morning it talked about how when we get sober we think we are fixed. But the truth is, as with any disease, it does not happen over night. A fortune cookie once said, "Your 3 best doctors are faith, time, and patience." If anyone knows me, I'm not the most patient person in the world...but am working on it every day. I keep trusting God to help me every day. Lord knows I can't do it by myself. One day at a time, I get stronger and happier. Each day I know myself better. And I'm ok with that.

Day 4

The other day I had someone ask me how long I was going to go to meetings? My reply was, "As long as I want to stay sober." My reasoning is, when people go to church and then become Christians, do they stop going to church? No. They continue to go for the fellowship with other Christians, to learn more, to learn how to live. Same thing with the AA program. Addicts don't go to meetings, admit they are an alcoholic/addict, then quit going because they are "healed." No one is ever cured. This is an evil disease, and needs constant work for it to work. In one of my reading this morning, there was a quote. "*May you live all the days of your life.*" –Jonathan Swift. When I first read it, I thought. Well, that's what we do, right? But then I started to really think about it. Not just to live, which could mean, go though the motions as each day passes. But to really LIVE. Yes, life is hard, but accepting that, makes it easier to go though. We can spend a lot of time avoiding the hardships of life, but we could be using that same energy to solving our problems. Life is short, so we need to take advantage of every moment we have and to love.

Day 5

I've been really busy recently. (Not to make excuses.) Busy doing "normal" things: working, making dinner, helping with homework, family time, etc. In the past, my life consisted of working, drinking, and complaining. Nothing was good enough, I never felt good. I was always tired, I was unhappy. Everyone and everything was a burden to me. What a waste of my life. It's crazy to think that I am so happy with my life now. And it is "normal" to anyone else. I am still living paycheck to paycheck, deciding which bill has to be paid first. But you know what? It could be worse. I could not have a job, not have a loving family, not have good friends that really care about me. I am so happy to be where I am today, because I've seen my rock bottom, and I don't ever want to go there again. I am so blessed. Also, I have some great news. My author's final proof of my book is in the mail!!! This is so real! I will actually have a copy in my hand next week. To give it the go-ahead to go into production. I am so amazed at how much my life has changed. And you know what? It didn't just happen, I had to work for it.

Day 6

I heard someone the other day say. "Why me? Why did I become an addict? I shouldn't be an addict." Well, I thought about it for a minute and realized, I didn't want to either, but people with cancer don't choose to have it either. We are dealing with a cunning, baffling, deadly disease. When I was younger, I didn't think, "Hey, when I grow up I want to be a doctor, oh wait no, I want to be an alcoholic." I didn't choose to become an addict, and I can't choose not to be an addict. I will always be an addict, but I am responsible for my recovery. I can choose what I do about it today. I can choose how I respond to different circumstances today. Before I would drink for any reason, like, "I had a bad day, I need a drink." or "Today was a great day, I need to celebrate!" Then everything became a reason to drink. It was sunny. It was cloudy. I was happy. I was sad. EVERYTHING. It was ridiculous. Now, I just celebrate life because God gave me one more day on this earth, alive and sober.

Day 7

It's a fantastically dreary day today again, as it has been all week. I'm patiently waiting for the sun to come back out. I saw a quote today that I liked.

"To err is human, but when the eraser wears out ahead of the pencil, you're overdoing it." –Josh Jenkins

It is so true. We all make mistakes, because we are human. But when we continue to make the same mistakes over and over and over again, there is a problem. We need to learn from our mistakes. We need to own them. With that, also, we are not perfect. We will still make them, and "bad" things still might happen to us, losing a job or someone we love. Sobriety doesn't make life perfect, but it does make it better than what it was. We will be better to deal with these issues, called life. We are capable of great things. We can be honest and caring if we choose to be.

Day 8

Today has been such a great day. I feel so blessed today. Such amazing things are happening in my life right now, that I never thought possible. I can't go in to any detail yet, but it will soon be revealed. :) Anyways! I saw a GREAT quote today.

"Acceptance does not mean that I have to agree, I don't have to approve. I don't even have to like it. I just have to accept." –unknown

Wow! This is so true. When I first got sober, I thought, "Wow, this is gonna suck." I thought it would be boring, I would have no friends. But it is the total opposite. The first thing I had to do was admit it. I knew I had a problem, I knew I needed help. I wanted help, but I didn't want it. Was it worth the energy? Did it really matter? I wasn't hurting anyone, but myself right? WRONG! I was hurting everyone. It was a disease that infected and affected everyone around me. Everyone that I was close to, everyone that really loved me. I didn't realize how everything I did affected everyone also. Now, it can be the same way. With my negativity, I was affecting everyone negatively. But now with my sobriety, I can affect positively as well. Do you know how good it feels to have someone say something as little as, "Lauren, watching you in your sobriety gives me hope." WOW! That feeling is amazing! Never in a million years would I have thought I would have a positive impact on someone else. To give someone else suffering from addiction, a little glimpse of hope. Showing someone that it's not so bad being sober! It's the best feeling in the world!

Day 9

A year ago, I would still be in bed, hiding my drinking, feeling like crap. Today I have gone to church, made lunch, and now am watching the Chicago Bears play or attempt to play....I am doing "normal" things. When I first got to AA, I was scared and alone. I felt the people there would look down at me, judge me. That was one of the reasons I didn't want to go to church. I was scared of what people would think of me. That they would think I was a "bad" person. Me saying all those things, was me being judgmental myself. I was judging those who I thought were judging me. How crazy is that! I needed to stop and think. Only God can judge me. I have no control over what people think of me. I can't change that. I can only change how I act, or react to that. But when I got sober, I didn't do it alone. I had a power greater than myself, whom I call God, carry me through the doors. I didn't know what to think at first. Was I going to talk, tell me people about myself? Tell them all my deepest darkest secrets? Were they going to talk to me? Once I heard others talk of their experiences, trials, triumphs, I felt more at ease. These people were like me. Hearing their stories, made me realize that they weren't doing it alone, and I couldn't either. I needed a higher power, God. I always had something that I was "worshipping." When I was drinking, it was alcohol. I always believed and knew there was a God, but wasn't always following the right path. The path I knew I should be on. I did what I wanted to. I would do anything for it, lie to get it, hide it. When I had it, and I would choose it over you in a heartbeat. Once I stopped worshipping that, I needed to find a power greater than myself, and that is God. So that is where I am today. Finding myself, and finding God. Only with His help, can I stay sober one more day!

Day 10

"Remember, today is the tomorrow you worried about yesterday." –Dale Carnegie

I'm always worrying about the future. Is what I planned going to happen? Is it going to be what I expected? Is it going to be worse? When? Why? What? AHHHHHH! In my sobriety I have learned to just take it easy. My worrying all the time about something I have no control over is pointless. It gets me nowhere except more frustrated. I have learned that I need to pray every morning and to give it to God. Whatever happens, happens. It's all in God's plan, so why am I so stressed about it. I'm not saying that life is perfect now, but is sure is a lot better. I know I can't do it alone. I've tried, by myself. It doesn't work. There has to be a power greater than myself that has control over everything I don't. So each morning, I pray for God's will. Whatever happens has a reason. It may not go with I think is good timing, or the way I think it should have happened. But God made it that way. Another thing I have to work on is patience. I want everything done yesterday. I need to work on being patient and trust in God's timing, and know that there is good reason it is like that. I work on these things daily, and will have to for the rest of my life.

Day 11

I got my author's proof in the mail and it's approved!!! It is now available for sale on createspace.com/4931083 or also on amazon.com. Search under books, then "From the Weeds" How exciting! It's amazing how so much had changed. It didn't come easy either. It takes work, but it is well worth it. Being able to enjoy doing homework with my daughter, playing dinosaurs with my son, is amazing. Being the mom I should be, the mom my kids deserve. Being a better wife to the husband I was blessed with who loves and supports me. Being a better daughter to my parents who I have put through so much turmoil, but have always given me unconditional love. I don't have really much today, just that I am very blessed and grateful to be a RECOVERING alcoholic/addict.

Day 12

Today I saw a quote and really love it.

"There is a huge difference between wanting to change and being willing to change. Almost everyone wants to change for the better. Very few are willing to take the steps necessary to create that change." –John T. Child

That is so true. Where I go to meetings, there is a sign up that says "YAGOTTAWANNA". You have to really make that decision and follow through with it. For a while, people told me how my life would be so much better if I stopped drinking, stopped using. When I thought of an alcoholic, I saw a homeless guy, with a brown bag, under the bridge. Not a woman, with a family, a job, and a car. I wasn't an alcoholic. I knew I had a problem, but thought it would be too hard to actually get better. I had to change, to actually be willing to. My excuse was that I didn't want to be away from my family, my kids. In all actuality, I wasn't really there anyways. I was physically, but not mentally or emotionally. So I had to go away to treatment for a bit. Some people can do it without detoxing. At least they didn't have to take that route. Eventually, we have to be honest with ourselves. We have to want it and do it. It works if you work it.

Day 13

"If you tell the truth, you don't have to remember anything." –Mark Twain

I love this quote from Mark Twain. When I was drinking and using, I had to remember everything. I was always telling one lie to cover another lie to cover another lie. I always had to remember exactly what I said earlier, so it wouldn't contradict what I already said. I had so many stories. Some I didn't even tell, but I had them in my head in case I was questioned. When I got sober I realized my life was a lie. It was just one after another. I would tell different people different things. When we start to lie it gets us closer to getting crazy again. Lying is what addicts do. Lying get us into trouble because we make secrets, which keeps us from others. We need to stay close to others to stay sober. A lie is just like a drink-you can't just have one.

Day 14

"Who had never tasted what is bitter, does not know what is sweet." –German Proverb

It's crazy that when I quit drinking, life got better. Maybe it is still the same, but when I quit drinking made me realize that life wasn't so bad. Before, I was upset about how we were barely making ends meet. But now I see it as, we both have jobs. I have had a lot more opportunities in my sobriety, and try to take advantage of each one I am given. I also started thinking about how it could be worse. Someone is always worse off than me. I am so blessed to have everything that I do have. I could have lost a lot more in my addiction. I'm lucky to still have a wonderful husband, 2 beautiful children, loving parents and family, and a job. I have heard of so many others who lost it all before they got sober. Some who lost it all, and died that way. And it hurts me to see others going down that same path, not knowing what is ahead of them. I can only speak of my experiences, to help someone else. Just to share my joys of sobriety and how life can and will get better, if the work is put into it.

Day 15

"Every experience, no matter how bad it seems, holds within it a blessing of some kind. The goal is to find it."
–Buddha

Today I want to talk about self-acceptance. In my addiction, I hated myself and everything I did. I didn't feel worthy of anything. Once I got sober, I had to realize that I wasn't a bad person. I had just done some bad things. Like Buddha said, "Every experience holds a blessing. You just need to find it." That's right along with everything happens for a reason or it's ok to make a mistake as long as you learn from it. NO one is perfect. We all make mistakes. But we need to find the good in it. I believe my experience with addiction has helped me be able to share my story with other addicts. Maybe my being open about it may help someone else want to get sober too. I want to lead by example. I want to share how life is so much better when we're sober, instead of wasting each day, waiting for the next, chasing that next high.

Day 16

"Once you have accepted your flaws, no one can use them against you." -unknown

I love this quote. I saw it on Facebook the other day and LOVE it. Once I got sober, I felt people would judge me for my past. Once I realized the path I took was the one God laid in front of me, I felt better. "Everything happens for a reason" and "I wouldn't be who I am today if I wouldn't have gone through what I went through." Once I accepted myself and what I had done, *only then* could I move forward. I could have sulked and felt sorry for myself, and hated myself for what I had done or I could learn from it, and grow. It was a hard thing to do. I knew I had a problem, but to actually admit it, accept it, and own it, and leave it behind, only then could I move forward. I felt as if a weight was lifted, I seriously do. I also don't really care what people think about me. I'm not out to please anyone else. I don't need to be accepted by others, I only need to accept myself.

Day 17

"God has perfect timing; never early, never late. It takes a little patience and faith, but it's worth the wait."

-unknown

I have a lot of things on my plate right now, and have a lot of hard decisions ahead of me: these are big life changing events. I keep praying for God to let me know what I should do, give me a sign. I want an answer now, not later. One thing I struggle with is patience. Patience is a big one. I want everything yesterday. Today is too late. It really isn't ever possible. I am working on being more patient and giving any situation I have to God. I have to trust in Him that his path is the right one, even though I think I have a better idea. Sometimes I'm wrong, but always think I need to be right. (ask my husband ☺)] But in the long run I do need to be patient, it will all work out...in God's time. It IS worth the wait.

Day 18

"God grant me the serenity to accept the things I cannot change, the courage to change the things I can, and the wisdom to know the difference." –Reinhold Niebuhr

When some people think of the Serenity Prayer, they automatically think of an addict. Before I got sober, when I heard that saying, I immediately thought of an alcoholic. That is was "their" motto. Now, I am one of "those people." In all actuality it can be used in everyday life. The definition of change is: the quality of mind or spirit that enables a person to face difficulty, danger, pain, etc., without fear; bravery. Change is a hard thing. When I got sober, I didn't just quit drinking, I had to change everything. Every aspect of my life has changed. My outlook on a lot of things is different too. I also had to realize what I CAN'T change. I can't change other people. The only thing I can change is my reaction to others. I needed to learn how to think things through before I say them, not just blow up and overreact. This is a continuing process. It's an everyday thing that I need to work on. Another quote I like is: "When you can't change the direction of the wind — adjust your sails" -H. Jackson Brown Jr.

Day 19

"Never be afraid to help others in their time of need.
You never know when you may need that shoulder to
lean on." -unknown

The best way to help yourself is by helping others. I like that quote. That is so true. I really understand that now. I was very selfish before, I didn't really care about anyone else. Now I just want to share my story and be able to help others in recovery, and those still struggling. I always have a hand out for anyone that needs help, needs someone to talk to. I am human and have problems too, and sure would like to have someone there for me in times of trouble. People talk about what goes around, comes around. It is true. Before, I didn't care about anyone so I had no one there for me. It was my own fault. I pushed everyone away. I was isolated. But being sober, I have gained new friends, real friends, ones that understand me, (as much as you can.) :) who really care about me and my sobriety, and I feel the same about them. So I am so much happier now, being negative only made everything around me negative. There was nothing positive about me or what I did. Being sober, and filling my life with joy, makes everything around me seem better too. Life is still hard, but someone always has it worse. When I am troubled I need to comfort someone more troubled. When I am lonely, there is always someone feeling lonelier. I just need to keep my head up, it will get better.

Day 20

"Whether you think can you can, or think you can't,
you're right." -Henry Ford

Today I saw something about optimism. I really like that little saying. Your perception of things has a lot to do with your attitude. Choosing to be optimistic just feels better. If I say I can't, there is no way I ever will, if I don't try. If I think I can, I will.

"Optimism is essential to achievement and is also the foundation of courage and true progress." -Nicholas Murray Butler

That is one thing I learned about recovery. If I choose to be negative and be a "sober drunk", I can't really be happy. If want to truly be a "recovering alcoholic", I need to be optimistic. Perception is a choice. I can choose to say a cup is half empty or half full, but technically it is full. 1/2 water and 1/2 oxygen. :) Every morning when my day starts, I need to smile, at least it is a good start. SMILE!

Day 21

"You live longer once you realize that any time spent being unhappy is wasted." –Ruth E. Renkle

I've been thinking about happiness. It is what you make of it. Time spent unhappy is time wasted. Here is another quote I like. "Happiness is appreciating what you have, not getting what you want." I have been happier now in my life than ever. I am so blessed with a wonderful husband and two great kids. They have loved me unconditionally. Happiness is a journey, not a destination. It is not a point that you get it to and that is it. It is an everyday thing. I am the only person that can make myself happy. I am ultimately responsible for how I feel. If I choose to be miserable in my life, that's where I will stay. If I choose to be happy, life will get better. I have nothing more now than I did when I was drinking, but I am happy. I am happy with what I do have, because I could have lost it all. I should have lost it all. But being in the place I was before, emotionally and psychologically, I was never going to be happy. I have full appreciation for what I have today. And I do not want to lose that.

Day 22

"Regret nothing. It makes you who you are." -unknown

I've been thinking a lot lately...I should have done this or why did I do that? What was I thinking? But you know what? It is what it is. There is nothing I can do about the past, so why waste my time wallowing in my self-pity, feeling sorry for myself, or regretting my past. Without my past I wouldn't be where I am today. I don't regret my past. I just regret the time wasted. I will never get back the time I wasted on doing nothing, and missing out on important "firsts." But I will take advantage of every moment I do have now. Another little quote... Look at life through the windshield, not the rear view mirror. The rear view mirror is there to remind us of where we have been, but we don't have to go back there. The windshield is larger than the rear view mirror, because that's where we are going. Well keep looking forward and have a great day!

Day 23

"Serenity is not the absence of conflict, but the ability to cope with it." -unknown

Life has gotten a lot better since I'm sober, but nothing around me has changed, I had to change. And with that change, came new opportunities. I recently had a book published, and someone asked me why my book wasn't in the order of my life. I didn't want people to think that since I got sober everything is perfect. It's not, but it's a heck of a lot better than it was. (Also, I didn't want people to kill themselves after reading the first few pages which are so depressing and suicidal.) Life is life. I also didn't want people to skip around, only reading the section on recovery. I want people to see my life as it was, the rollercoaster of emotions, or lack thereof. I had some great experiences in my life when I was using, and I've had some bad times now that I'm sober. The quote above, brings it all together. Having serenity does not mean I don't still have struggles, but I now can deal with them in a different way...a much better way.

Day 24

"The only person you should try to be better than, is the person you were yesterday." –unknown

I really like the above quote. Strive for progress, not perfection. I know I will not ever be perfect, but as long I am a better person than I was yesterday, I feel I have gotten somewhere. I don't want to be anyone else. I just want to be me. I don't hate the person I am today, but want to become a better person every day; to be less selfish, to be a better listener, to be more kind, to be more loving. The way I was headed before, was either nowhere or down. I didn't care about anyone but me, but then it got to the point where I wasn't even doing that. Now I put one foot in front of the other, and have a positive outlook, because you know what...I only live once, so why have it be miserable. I'm not going to get another chance at it. It's not like when I die, I start a new life.....

Day 25

"Courage is what it takes to stand up and speak. Courage is also what it takes to sit down and listen." -Winston Churchill

I have come to learn that I am courageous in standing up for what I believe in and being open about speaking, but what I really need to work on is just being quiet and listening. Sometimes I get so caught up in telling my story by not being quiet and listening to others. That is one thing I am continuously working on. I have always been a good talker, but really need to slow down, be patient, and listen to others. Sometimes, just listening is all someone needs. They don't want to hear me ramble on about my problems. They just want someone to listen; someone to hear what's going on in their life. Just letting them speak it out in words, instead of hearing it in their own head, may make more sense once the words come out. So today I will be still, sit down and listen.

Day 26

"There is a difference between truly listening and waiting for your turn to talk." -Ralph Waldo Emerson

Wow, this quote really got me. I know now that I need to start listening more and talking less, but this quote is spot on. There is a BIG difference between hearing and listening. According to Wikipedia, "Listening is often confused with hearing. While hearing is a process that can be scientifically explained, listening is a neurological cognitive regarding the processing of auditory stimuli received by the auditory system." So I need to shut up and listen. I need to really listen to them, how they are feeling, what their hurts are. Maybe I don't need to say a word at all, but I need to really listen to them, instead of just hearing the words that come out of their mouths. I'll be honest sometimes I am more apt to listen to someone just so they will listen to me, but I need to be genuinely listening, and genuinely caring. So with that being said, I will shut up, and listen to you. Enough about me...tell me about you...

Day 27

"One day at a time" -unknown

Today marks 9 months of sobriety time! That is so awesome. But you know what? It's no any longer than anyone else. It's just another 24 hours. I can't look too far into the future, because I am just 1 drink away from being a drunk. It could be any day. I'm not promised another day of sobriety none the less another day alive. I have to just put one foot in front of the other and do it one day at a time. Here is my poem called "One Day at a Time"

One Day at a Time

You were my best friend.
I loved you so.
I would do anything,
To any lengths I would go.

I would lie to people about you,
To the people closest to me.
You said you'd always be there,
Always make me happy.

They said you would kill me.
You'd take all I cared for.
I just couldn't believe that.
You said you could give me more.

But then they said they'd leave me
If you were who I chose.
Were you really worth it?
Were you worth all these woes?

So I sat back to think
Of all the hurt you caused me.
Not one thing I did better with you
On that we could agree.

Before you took me to the grave.
Before you took everything.
I tore from the grip you had on me
But to me you tried to cling.

Now I live without you
I'm trying to realign
Doing the next right thing.
One day at a time.

So with that being said. I'm very proud of myself, but it's just one more day! And that's all I can keep doing!

Day 28

"I'm learning to love myself. It's the hardest thing I've done." -unknown

One thing I have always struggled with is loving myself, being happy with who I am. I have always felt like somewhat of a failure. I was good in sports and did well in school, but inside always felt defeated. I was never pretty enough, or whatever. I have never felt beautiful. People would say that, but I always thought they were just being nice. But in all actuality, what is pretty? Who are the "pretty police?" What am I really trying to attain? Who am I trying to please? The only person I really can please is myself. When I was drinking and such, I hid all my true feeling, I didn't want to feel, like the crappy person I was. Now, I have learned to forgive myself, and truly love myself. If I don't love myself, who else will. I have also been more aware of this, having a daughter. Growing up is hard as it is, nonetheless kids being mean and judging you. I need to show her she is beautiful, and make her feel and truly believe it. I need to stop being hard on myself, telling myself I'm fat. If she hears me say that, what is she going to do if she gains a few pounds? Lose all self-esteem? Feel like crap, because she thinks she is "fat." Having a daughter has really made me think of how what I do can REALLY affect others. So today I feel beautiful and am happy to be me!

Day 29

"In life, we never lose friends, we only learn who the true ones are." -unknown

I've really been thinking a lot about friends. I thought I lost some friends when I was really drinking, and lost some too when I quit. But maybe they weren't really friends. Not a lot of people stuck around during my excessive drinking. And if you are reading this and feel guilty, I'm sorry. It is what it is. If you don't want to be friends with me, I can't make you. I have learned what real friends are. And now I am finding and making real friends. Real friends are those who genuinely care about me, who listen to me, and who I want to listen to as well. No offense to anyone, but not just a drinking buddy. I am not saying I didn't enjoy my time with you. That was my lifestyle then, and that's what I wanted. I just wanted someone to drink with. And I didn't really have "problems" or "feeling" to share, I was drinking them away. I didn't want to deal with them. So with that being said, *"A real friend is one who walks in when the rest of the world walks out."* -Walter Winchell.

Day 30

"Before you judge me, make sure that you are perfect."
-unknown

Since I've been in recovery, I have been worried about people judging me. According to Webster's dictionary to judge means "to form an opinion about through careful weighing of evidence and testing of premises." So judging really can't be done unless you know someone very well and have heard his or her whole story. Once you have heard their story, it will more sense. So in all actuality, no one can "really" judge me, but God, because He is perfect. And He will judge me fairly. He knows I am not perfect. I am human, for if I were perfect, I would not be human. I have also learned that I cannot judge others either. I need to be less critical. Who am I to talk? I have made a lot of bad decisions. I have gone down a lot of wrong roads, but I have also done a lot of good things. Just because I was drinking and such, doesn't make me a bad person, I just made some bad decisions. So who am I to give advice? I cannot and should not tell anyone what they should or should not do, only tell about my personal experience and opinions. So with you I share my blog.

Day 31

"I'm sober, not boring!" -unknown

Some people I used to hang out with haven't invited me to hang out since I got sober. I don't know if they think that I think I am better than them or that I don't like people that drink. It's not that at all. I just can't drink, because I can't just have one, or just drink socially, I take it to a whole other level. Or maybe they think I am boring, or dull. I am still fun. I am actually more fun, because I don't get loud and do stupid things like I used to do. And just because I quit drinking doesn't mean I sit in my house all day and judge the world. I do fun stuff, with my family, with my kids, friends. We go hiking, swimming, and fishing. This summer we had a "Summer '14 Bucket List." It consisted of 75 fun things to do during the summer. Just enjoying the world, and those I care about, instead of wasting my time and energy and not remembering a lot of stuff. I have learned to have fun without being wasted. If you think sobriety is boring, you are not doing it right! ☺

Day 32

"Friends become our chosen family." -unknown

I am so blessed to have so many people who really care about me. I have gained a lot of new, true friends in recovery. A lot of the people I met in treatment, I consider family. They were there with me to start this new chapter in my life. I continue to talk to a lot of them on a regular basis. We are all connected, in that were all lost, but trying to find ourselves. I have chosen some pretty cool people to call family! Good friends are like stars, you can't always see them, but you know they are always there. There are some people in recovery that I may be able to talk to more easily because they have been where I have been. I couldn't "connect" with someone who is suffering from a fatal illness, like cancer, or give comfort to someone who had lost a parent or child, in the way that one who has "been there" could. But put me in the room with another alcoholic/addict, and we could talk all day long. I'm not saying I don't have any good communication skills with those who are not addicts. I can talk to anyone. But it IS easier to talk to someone when you've walked in their shoes. I am learning to communicate better in general.

Day 33

"The 'I' in illness is isolation, and the crucial letters in wellness is 'we'." -unknown

I have learned that being alone and being lonely are two completely different things. If you can be comfortable with yourself by yourself, you are not lonely. When I was drinking, I was lonely and isolated myself. I avoided going to family functions, to friend's houses, anything. I didn't want to be around anyone else, none the less myself. I was sulking in my own miserableness. I had to learn to ask others for help. "We gradually and carefully pull ourselves out of the isolation and loneliness of addiction and into the mainstream of life." (p. 35 Alcoholics Anonymous.) I need the fellowship of other people to continue getting better. I cannot do it alone. There is another little saying I like. "You are confined only by the walls you build yourself." Here is a poem I wrote.

the wall

i've been hiding
won't let you in
brick by brick
building this wall
burying my soul
now cautiously
removing each

I felt so alone, but I built the wall myself, and now must slowly tear it down brick by brick.

Day 34

I have been thinking a lot about 'crying out for help.' When I was younger, I was secretly crying out for help. I was silent and wrote depressing, suicidal poems about it. Some were pretty dark, but that was how I felt. I'm just glad it didn't actually get that far. Everyone cries out for help in a different way, a lot of the time though, it is through silence. No one cared about my problems, so why share them with anyone. It was life and my messed up head. It wasn't anyone's business. And no one would ever be able to talk to me about it. They would be doctors, who knew the "book" side of it, but not the "heart" side of it. They were going to tell me how to feel, or what I should feel. No one REALLY knew how I felt or could really help me. Now today, I know that there is light at the end of the tunnel, I just had to reach for it. If I reach my hand out for help, there will be someone there to hold it. I couldn't have done it alone. But now today, I am a very blessed woman, who wouldn't change anything, it makes me who I am today. And I am stronger for that. Here is a poem I wrote.

The Writing on the Wall

As she wrote them in her closet,
and on the walls of her bedroom.
The "acceptable" ones were available for all to see.
They were convincingly composed by a seemingly cheery individual.
While hidden in the closet was the truth.
There she wrote the anguished,
cynical thoughts and feelings of reality.
Others were blind to her true behavior.
Her anxious demeanor was buried in lies.
On the outside was a bright, easygoing soul.
A humorous, quirky character.
She knew not the blessings before her,
so kept holding on to the contradictive manor of her ways.
For many years she continued this.
When will the truth be told?
Or will it ever.

With that being said, listen to the silence you may be hearing from someone you love or care about. They may be calling out for help, so <u>really listen</u> to them.

Day 35

"There IS a light at the end of the tunnel, but you'll have to keep moving forward to get there." -unknown

Yesterday, I talked about crying out for help. It's along that same line today. Life can seem so dark at times, like the pain will never end. I feel like I'm going the wrong way. I have taken so many wrong turns. There is no way my life could get better. I've made so many mistakes. There is no hope. I have all these thoughts running through my head. But I need to stop and think a second, and look forward. I can only go forward to the light. If I turn around, it will only stay dark. I have to keep moving though, toward the light. Things will get better. I don't have to stay stuck in my misery. But if I sit here in the dark, and don't move at all, it will never get better. I have to put one foot in front of the other to get somewhere. There is an acronym for HOPE. Hang On Pain Ends. It can only stay dark for so long. There is another little quote I like. "If there's no light at the end of the tunnel, march on down there and turn it on yourself." -Patricia Morse. The light doesn't just happen; you have to go towards it. Here's a little poem I wrote.

Inevitable

The rain is cold and dreary, yes,

But soon the storm is done.

The cold dark night surrounds me now,

Yet the warmth of the sun is soon to come.

So keep your head up, and keep on keeping on…

Day 36

"It's just a bad day, not a bad life." -unknown

I have been talking about depression and being down, and getting back up. Now that I'm sober, my life has gotten better. Not perfect but a lot better. I still have bad days, but I need to look at it this way. It's one day. Tomorrow is a new day, so just make it through this day, and enjoy the good in it. And you know what? In a few days or weeks, I probably won't even remember it. Now some days I will never forget, losing a loved one, losing a job or what not. But a lot of the "bad" days, just aren't as good as we expected. Sometimes we expect every day to be fantastic and amazing. But in reality, it's life. We all have our ups and downs. There are some people who we think have it all, all the money, all the friends, fancy cars, and fancy houses. We think their life is perfect. But look at Robin Williams, he had it all, or so we thought. He had everything, but his true happiness. When you take away all the material things, he is just like us. Another human being trying to make it through it this thing we call life. And we only have one shot at it, so why not enjoy the ride. So keep your head up!

Day 37

"Be strong enough to stand alone, smart enough to know when you need help, and brave enough to ask for it."
–Ziad K. Abdelnour

Asking for help is one of the hardest things to do. Sometimes we know we need help, but are too afraid to ask. Katrina Mayer said, "*I'm courageous enough to know I can accomplish great things. I'm humble enough to know when to ask for help.*" That is so true. Asking for help is not a sign for weakness. It shows that you know you can do it, but need a hand to hold. Anything is easier when someone, a friend or God, is there by your side. Even if they aren't doing anything or saying anything, you know you are not alone. Life can be scary sometimes, but you always have a friend to stand with if you just ask. Maybe that person was too afraid to ask you. And you just helped them too without even knowing it. Here is another poem I wrote.

Friend

I love how you don't judge me.
You have been in my shoes.
You were always there to listen.
When I had nothing to lose.

I live like there's no tomorrow.
I enjoy every moment alive.
You've taught me to be happy.
I feel so revived.

So thank you for always being there.
And extending out your hand.
To help me up when I fell down.
And hold me steady when I stand.

Day 38

"Learn from yesterday, live for today, hope for
tomorrow." –Albert Einstein

I know we all make mistakes, we are human. We need to learn from them, live for today, because that is all we have, and tomorrow is not promised. Complaining about yesterday doesn't make today any better. We need to make the best of today. Enjoy the life we have, the little things of today will be the big things of yesterday. Life is short, so live it. We need to enjoy the people we love, let them enjoy us. We may not know what me mean to others. I need to be the reason someone smiles. So if you are reading this, smile! :) That is at least one happy memory for today. I hope you enjoy reading these. I enjoy writing them. And if I can help one person make it through today, it is a good day. To let someone know they are not alone, they are not crazy. I think it's interesting when people say they are "different," it is used as a bad connotation. Different than what. What is "normal?" Normal is boring. So then I want to be different. Anyways, that is a topic for another day. :) Here is a short poem I wrote.

Tomorrow

I live for what is now.
The next day is not here,
nor promised.
And you?

Day 39

"Thanks to those who hated me, you made me stronger. Thanks to those who loved me, you made my heart grow fonder. Thanks to those who cared, you made me feel important. Thanks to those who entered my life, you made me who I am today. Thanks to those who left, you showed me that nothing lasts forever. Thanks to those who stayed, you showed me true friendship. Thanks to those who listened, you made me feel like I was worth it." -unknown

It is almost Thanksgiving, and I am remembering all the things I need to be thankful for, and it's mostly people. I really am so thankful for all the people that stuck by me through all the crap recently: those who loved me when I didn't love myself, those who cared about me when I didn't care. I am also thankful for all the people, positive and negative, for you have made me who I am today. I am so very thankful for all the people who have come into my life through recovery. Those who have been where I have been, and are there with me moving forward. And for those who have stayed there through it all. There are some people who aren't there anymore, and I am partially to blame, because I didn't care. I am very grateful for my life that I have today. My family and friends, new and old, I thank you, and I can't thank you enough. You have made me a stronger woman today. Sometimes I am thankful, but don't say anything. I think they just know. So again I say thank you. So thank someone you love today! I'm sure they don't hear it enough.

Day 40

"Never look down on someone unless you're helping them up."–Jesse Jackson

We don't ever need to look down on anyone. We are all equals. Some may have more material things than others, but that means nothing. We cannot take anything with us when we die. It is all in in your heart and soul. *"Our prime purpose in this life is to help others. And if you can't help them, at least don't hurt them."* -Dalai Lama. So if you are going to be selfish and not help others, don't be mean or knock them down. They are or have been down, and are looking to get up, or looking for a hand to get up. <u>Helping others is the most humbling thing.</u> I have been trying to do the next right thing, and help someone else. I have had so many others help me through my struggles, it is about time I do the service and help someone else. We really shouldn't need a reason to help people. Helping others is a great way to help ourselves. Here is a brevity poem about altruism or selflessness.

Someday

You go out of your way
to help me,
yet it hurts you.
Why?
You are a gift
from God.
Thank you.
I will
pay it forward...
someday.

Day 41

"Being hurt is something you can't stop from happening, but being miserable is always your choice." -unknown

When I was drinking, I was miserable, miserable about everything. Nothing made me happy. And it was everyone else's fault. I wanted everything my way, and I wanted it now. I thought everything made me miserable!!! But, I was making myself miserable. No one else was!!! AND I was hurting so many others. And as I'm sure you have heard. *"Misery loves company."* I was making everyone around me miserable. I was hurting them. Today, I feel terrible for what I have done, or not done. I will never be able to make up those firsts that I missed. You will see in the following poem, how I really felt. I had put myself into the hole I dug, and I thought I should stay there. Now I am enjoying every moment alive. I don't want to hurt anyone anymore, only help.

Misery

I am comfortable in my "little world."

I've been stuck here so long

I don't know

if I can ever get out.

Or if I really want to.

I enjoy drinking every day.

Getting sick all the time.

Getting sick from drinking too much.

From not drinking.

I enjoy being hopeless.

For hating my job.

My boss.

My life.

I am comfortable

in my misery.

I have caused it.

So I should suffer.

I enjoy missing

family functions.

Dinners.

Family reunions.

Cookouts.

Christmas'.

I can't be gone

long enough to not drink.

Or I will get sick.

Or someone will notice.

I enjoy only getting 1/2 a paycheck,

because I missed work.

I have a headache.

My stomach hurts.

My throat hurts.

I lie. To you.

To everyone.

To myself.

I enjoy missing

important moments

in my children's lives.

Their first day of kindergarten.

First t-ball game.

First recital.

I enjoy blaming my husband for everything.

For what he didn't do right.

Or what he didn't do at all.

I enjoy losing the trust of my family.

Mom.

Dad.

Husband.

Children.

I enjoy this misery.

So here I shall stay.

Day 42

"The moment that you start to wonder if you deserve better, you do." -unknown

I used to think I deserved what I had. I deserved to be miserable because of what I had done or not done. I didn't deserve to be happy. But, the moment I decided **that I did deserve better; to be happy;** it wasn't only about what I deserved, **it was about my family.** My kids didn't deserve to lose their mom when they were 6 and 2, because of her drinking. Being absent from her first recital, her first t-ball game. My husband didn't deserve to have a wife that didn't care, that didn't act like a "wife." Last year, at school he looked like a single father. HE was the one going to her parent/teacher conferences. HE was the one picking her up at the bus stop. They deserved better, to be happy. Now I am doing to what I can to make them happy, to make me happy. To do what is best for my family. I had to learn that my past was the past and I didn't want to be miserable for the rest of my life. So one day at a time, I will make my life better, and be happy. Happiness is appreciating what you have, not getting what you want.

Day 43

"It is not happy people who are thankful. It is thankful people who are happy." -unknown

I have been so grateful for everything I have. I have nothing more than when I was drinking except my sanity. Yet I have so much more. I am so grateful for my family and those still in my life. I really like the above quote. I used to think if I had more I would be happy. But now I am so thankful for what I do have, and I am so much happier. There is always something to be thankful for. Be thankful for what you have, and you'll end up having more. If you concentrate on what you don't have, you will never ever have enough. Thanksgiving is tomorrow and I am realizing that I am truly grateful for many things. Every Thanksgiving we go around the table and say one thing we are happy for, and I would usually just say "friends and family." But now I am so grateful for so much more, remembering each person individually not just a group of people. Just realizing each breath is a gift, each memory I have is a blessing. So be thankful today, for all you have.

Day 44

"If the only prayer you ever say in your whole life is 'thank you', that would suffice." –Meister Eckhart

HAPPY THANKSGIVING! Lately I have realized that I don't really need to ask God for anything. He provides me with everything I need. I just need to thank Him. Every day I am more blessed. I am so grateful for everything God has done for me. Some people might think, me thanking God for EVERYTHING is crazy, but I am. I have put myself in some bad situations, but God has always had my back. He is always there to pick me back up. So today, I am truly grateful for God's forgiveness. For always being there, for loving me unconditionally. And I will continue to thank Him everyday for His abundant blessings. Have a safe and Happy Thanksgiving! Enjoy this time with your family, as you are too blessed.

Day 45

"It's okay to be sad sometimes." -unknown

I always talk about perception and how you need to be happy, but life isn't perfect and you will have times when you are sad. There are times in life where you should feel sad; like losing a friend or someone you love, or anything you cared for. But there is a difference between being sad and depression. There is also a difference between being alone and isolation. Sometimes when you are sad you just want to be alone, that is fine. You just need to make sure you don't do it forever. Life does go on. Sometimes you want to talk about it sometimes you don't, but in the end you should "vent" somehow. You could do it through music, or writing, or whatever you enjoy doing. You may feel sad, but little by little you will feel better. Feeling sad is part of life. It is good that you are feeling too. Feeling is what I was hiding with drinking. I didn't want to feel. It's hard learning to feel again, and sometimes those feeling I don't want to feel. I want everything to be fine and dandy. But without the sad times, I would appreciate the happy times as much. So keep your head up!

Day 46

"Let your smile change the world, but don't let the world change your smile." -unknown

Yesterday was a sad but true post so today I am going to cheer it up a little. I really like this little saying. Your smile should be able to affect people, but don't let the world change yours. A smile is the most beautiful curve on a woman's body, so flaunt it. I feel better about myself, just smiling. I'm never fully dressed without smiling in the mirror first. :) That completes my outfit, and I always seem to look better with a smile on my face. I know some days we fake a smile just to get through it, but a real one is so much better. A smile is infectious. If you can smile, and make someone else smile, maybe they will do the same for someone else. So smile at someone today. Maybe that is just what they needed. That's all for today! ☺

Day 47

"If you want your children to turn out well, spend out twice as much time with them and half as much money."
–Abigail Van Buren

I've been very thankful this Thanksgiving season. And now it's Christmas time. I have been spending more quality time with my family. It is so much better for my children and myself, to spend quality time with them. They will remember the fun times we had, hiking or fishing or just playing outside on the swing set more than the Barbie I got her or the Thomas the Train pillow. But in the long run, memories are what they will remember. *"Children are like wet cement. Whatever falls on them makes an impression."* –Dr. Haim Ginott. This year I have been buying more gifts for them that are special to them, something personal or fun to do. Laney has been helping me wrap presents. I am showing her how, just like my mom taught me, so someday, she can teach her daughter. I want her to be able to teach her children the way to do things. I am so thankful to be able to do that. I wrote a poem this summer just watching her swing, just enjoying being a child. :)

Swing

I watch my daughter
play on her swing set.
She loves to swing.
She leans back
to feel breeze in her hair.
It blows back and forth
opposite movement of her legs.
She smiles with her eyes closed
as the sun reflects off her face,
then a tree shadows her
only for a moment.
Her bare feet graze
what's left of grass
on a path under her swing.
She could swing all day,
if I would let her....
"Time for dinner!"

So enjoy ever second you have with those you love.

Day 48

"The tallest oak in the forest was once just a little nut
that held its ground." -unknown

Don't give up!! The beginning is always the hardest. I have been thinking a lot about my book and myself. People ask how the book sales are going and they are going good! When you are getting ready to get a book published, all you can think about is have a million copies sold, now. But you have to start somewhere. J. K. Rowling had to sell her 1st copy of her 1st book. It took time to sell it. She didn't sell a million copies overnight. (Well, more recently she actually she did) :) but you know what I mean. She had to start at the bottom like everyone else. She had to work at it. Every accomplishment begins with the decision to try.

Day 49

"Live as if you were to die tomorrow. Learn as if you were to live forever." –Ghandi

As some of you may know, I just got a new job. I was excited about getting a new, more challenging job. I was still learning every day, but knew I had more potential. So, I am continually learning at this position now. I really thought this quote was particularly good for today, since this is my 3rd day at my new job. I want to learn, and am excited about this new opportunity. So, I will continue to live for today, and take everything I can from it, to learn more everyday as if I will live forever. It is not a good day if I didn't learn anything. There is another saying I like, "Learn from yesterday, live for today, hope for tomorrow." It is a lot like the other one. So pretty much, in the short, live and learn. So off to work I go, to cram by brain full of more information.

Day 50

"The couples that are "meant to be" are the ones who go through everything that is meant to tear them apart and come out even stronger than they were before."
-unknown

I am so blessed to have my husband by my side. He stayed with me and loved me when I didn't love myself. A reporter asked an old couple "How did you manage to stay together so long?" She replied, "It's simple really. We are from a time where if something is broke we fix it...not throw it away!" I feel sometimes we are supposed to go through some bad stuff to enjoy the good, even better. I love my husband so much. A perfect marriage is two imperfect people who refuse to give up on each other. Our marriage has grown stronger. I feel terrible for being a "bad" wife. I didn't care. So here is a poem I wrote while in my recovery.

Chris

I saw,
I craved,
I wanted,
you.

I adored,
I caressed,
I pleased,
you.

I broke,
I hurt,
I pained,
you.

I deprived,
I depressed,
I failed,
you.

I bettered,
I renewed,
I changed,
for you.

You embraced,
you loved,
you forgave,
me.

I love you.
Forever and always...

Day 51

"If you really want to do something, you'll find a way. If you don't, you'll find an excuse." –Jim Rohn

I have come to the realization that I want to be sober, I now stay sober because I want to not because someone is making me. It is not forced, and I don't hate dong it. I enjoy enjoying life, remembering it, making fun memories with my children. If you really want to do something, you will make it happen. No one can do that for you. I can just be me. People are going to judge me either way. People are always judging, so there is nothing I can change about someone's feelings. I can only change myself. I was so sick of making excuses for everything. For not going somewhere, for not saying something right, for everything. I didn't want to do anything and I made an excuse for it. But I wanted to get sober bad enough, so I did it. Well, am doing it. :) One day at a time. So keep your head up. If you want something bad enough, go after it. Do it. You can!

One day at a time

You were my best friend.
I loved you so.
I would do anything,
To any lengths I would go.

I would lie to people about you,
To the people closest to me.
You said you'd always be there,
Always make me happy.

They said you would kill me.
You'd take all I cared for.
I just couldn't believe that.
You said you could give me more

But then they said they'd leave me
If you were who I chose.
Were you really worth it?
Were you worth all these woes?

So I sat back to think
Of all the hurt you caused me.
Not one thing I did better with you
On that we could agree.

Before you took me to the grave.
Before you took everything.
I tore from the grip you had on me
But to me you tried to cling.

Now I live without you
I'm trying to realign
Doing the next right thing.
One day at a time.

Day 52

"It's better to feel pain that nothing at all."
–The Lumineers

One of the hardest things for me to do when I was getting sober was feeling again. I was hiding all my real feeling with my drinking. I guess I still had feelings, like sad, depressed, and lonely, but wasn't really feeling them. I was numbing them. I would have rather felt nothing than anything, good or bad. Sometimes paper was the only thing that would listen to me, or that I wanted to listen to me. I would write, happy or sad. Then it got to the point where I didn't even want to tell the paper anymore. It was hard for me to put feeling into words so that anyone could understand. But in sobriety I have learned to feel again, not that I really had a choice. :) But when they came, they all came at once. Feelings I hadn't felt in a long time. I was feeling regret, love, hope, sad, excited, nervous, ecstatic, overjoyed, and blessed…all at the same time. A friend of mine called it the "tornado effect". (Thanks Nina!) It was hard to sort out my feelings. I had hidden or masked them for so long. The smile on my face was holding back the tears in my heart. So I am glad to say that I am glad I feel again, good and bad. The bad feelings make the good, better. Here is a poem I wrote. It may have been posted on here before.

The Writing on the Wall

As she wrote them in her closet,
and on the walls of her bedroom.
The "acceptable" ones were available for all to see.
They were convincingly composed by a seemingly cheery individual.
While hidden in the closet was the truth.
There she wrote the anguished,
cynical thoughts and feelings of reality.
Others were blind to her true behavior.
Her anxious demeanor was buried in lies.
On the outside was a bright, easygoing soul.
A humorous, quirky character.
She knew not the blessings before her,
so kept holding on to the contradictive manor of her ways.
For many years she continued this.
When will the truth be told?
Or will it ever.

Day 53

"Peace-it does not mean to be in a place where there is no noise, trouble, or hard work. It means to be in the midst of those things and still be calm in your heart."
-unknown

My heart has been more at peace since I give every day to God. The world still goes on around me. I can just deal with it better now. I used to be so worried about what was going to happen next, or what was not going to happen. I tried to have control over everything in my life, when in reality the only thing I really had control over my actions and my reactions. A friend of mine, I will call S. always used to talk about "keeping his side of the street clean." It took me a while to get it. But there is another saying I saw that helped it make sense. *"Forgive others, not because they deserve forgiveness, but because you deserve peace."* I used to think I deserved all the crap I put myself through, but I deserve peace, and I am the only one that can give it to myself. As Ralph Waldo Emerson said, "Nobody can bring you peace, but yourself." So I wrote a poem about what is peace to me. It is an acrostic.

PEACE

Personally,
Eliminating
Alcohol
Changed
Everything

Peace means something different to everyone. When I was drinking, I never knew true peace. In sobriety, I am living it more each day.

Day 54

"In order to change, we must be sick and tired of being sick and tired." -unknown

Today something happen that I had not experienced yet in sobriety. I was sick all night, I mean all night. I could get out of bed to go to work. Lying in bed today for hours and hours made me really think of how "sick" I was. I was so used to throwing up multiple times a day, it was "normal" for me. I was so used to being miserable, that was all I knew. I'm sitting here typing, ashamed of how I used to be. My daughter has her Christmas program at school tonight. I still feel like crap, but I will be there for her this year. I can't imagine being like this all day every day. I would work like this, because I had to. If I missed work, I would lose money on my paycheck, and that bought my alcohol. So "Ya do what ya gotta do!" I don't ever want to go back to the way things were. I had to get to the point where I was sick and tired of being sick and tired to be able to change. Well, I got to that point. So here I am today, reminiscing of how miserable I was, and how happy I am now. So even though I am really "sick" today, I don't want to be "sick" again.

Day 55

"Emotionally, physically, and mentally tired." -unknown

Yesterday, I was sick. Today I feel better, but not great. I did a lot of thinking while lying in bed yesterday, not being able to sleep when I should have been. I was thinking of all the times I was sick. I was so sick physically AND mentally. The physical sickness was a norm. I had learned how to deal with puking and headaches, but the whole, nothing going on in my head and emotions, or lack thereof, all across the board was making me crazy. I was getting emotionally exhausted. I had felt nothing for so long, I had nowhere to go. I had hit bottom. Like I said yesterday, I had to get sick and tired of being sick and tired, before I was ever going to change anything. It was the hardest decision in my life I had ever had to make, but the best one. And now I have more emotions I know what to do with, which is a good thing. I am feeling. I am human again, and with that so comes life: good and bad, triumphs and struggles. It feels good to feel again.

Day 56

"One day you'll just be a memory for some people. Do your best to be a good one." -unknown

I have been thinking, once again, (I do a lot of that now days), about myself and how I will be remembered. A year ago, I know I wouldn't have been remembered well. People would have thought, "That girl killed herself, with alcohol." No one would really feel bad; they would think I deserved it. But now I feel, I have had a more positive affect on people in my life. People would remember me with a smile, not a grimice. I know this is kind of morbid today, but before I didn't really think I was going to die. Doctors told me MANY times alcohol was going to kill me, and I really didn't think it would happen to me. God really had his hand in that, because many times I should have. Now, I am more realistic, and know that it is inevitable, but want to leave a "good" footprint on this earth. I want to be remembered happy, humbled and blessed, not sad, sick and sorry. I am glad today to say that I think I have changed the thought of me. I know this is a weird topic today, but it's real. So with that being said, I'm grateful for one more day alive and sober. By the way, today is

10 MONTHS SOBER!!!!!

Day 57

"It's never too late–never too late to start over, never too late to be happy." –Jane Fonda

I've realized it's never too late to change. For some it may take longer than others, but only YOU can make that change. No one else can make it for you. I was unhappy and miserable, but I had to change before anything else was going to change. Happiness is appreciating what you have, not getting what you want. I have learned to be truly happy. I am so blessed with a loving family. That's all I need to be happy. People I love surrounding me. I don't need material things. Yeah, they are nice, but I don't need them to be truly happy. When I'm happy, I can make others around me happy too. When I was miserable, I made everyone around me miserable. Misery loves company. Once I got off my butt and out of my pity party, I had to work hard to find myself. Without me taking care of myself, I couldn't take care of anyone around me. It may sound selfish that I had to take care of me first, but it's the truth. There was no way I could be a good mom, be a good wife, or anything without being good to myself first. So if you aren't happy with the way things are now, do

something about it. It's better late than never, but really
never too late

Day 58

"You are not alone." -unknown

When I was drinking and using, I felt very alone. I pretty much did it to myself, I was isolating myself. When I got sober, I was worried I was going to start and continue this journey alone as well. I never realized how many other people feel the same way. When we get together physically or even online, we are together. I know I can do this. I see people that are living sober every day. They are not just NOT drinking, they are enjoying life sober. If I ever need to talk to someone, there are so many people I can talk to. I have recently joined some closed recovering groups on Facebook. There are SO many people just like me. Most I have never met, but can talk to on the same level, because they have been where I have been, and are where I am now. I am not alone one this journey of recovery. If you are struggling today, know that you are not alone. You matter so much. Don't give up. The hardest thing is to ask someone for help. But that is what we are here for, to help each other; to grow and mature and be a gift to one another. And if you are physically alone, know that God is with you. He will never leave your side. Know you care, and you matter!

Day 59

"Here's to many more firsts and many more great memories." –Christine Feehan

I have said it before about how I missed some "firsts". But I can't look back. I can only make new firsts now. Today, I am at my first book signing! I had my first sober Thanksgiving in a long time. I am now excited to have my first Christmas in a long time too. We had the most fun summer ever. We had a bucket list of 75 things to do. It was a blast! We are making the most fun memories. Looking back now, when I was a kid, all I remember are the good times. I guess it was because I had a lot. This first year of sobriety is going to be alot of firsts. I didn't celebrate my birthday this year, I was in treatment. So in February, I will celebrate my 1st birthday sober in a LONG time. New Year's, too. So I am actually excited this year. I'm ready and blessed to have the opportunity to enjoy these firsts.

Day 60

"We make a living by what we get, but we make a life by what we give."–Winston Churchill

I have thought about how much more I have now, (not material things) but true relationships. I feel so much more blessed. I never understood how truly blessed I am. I have so much to give, I want to give it away. I really like the quote above. My life is more full by what I can give back; to help someone else, in a time of need or to talk to them, or just to listen. Maybe that's all they want, an ear to listen. But I feel so much more full when I am giving it away. Sobriety, in the beginning, is selfish. I had to take care of myself before I could anyone else. Now that I have found myself, it's time for me to share this wonderful gift. Acts 20:35 says, "It is more blessed to give than to receive." So true. ...and it seems the more I give, the more I receive!!!

Day 61

"I'm no therapist, but I promise you this: I will listen. I will care." -unknown

I have been learning that the world does not revolve around me. I am not the center of the universe. But I am here to make my footprint on this earth. I want to be able to help others, by giving myself. Like the above phrase says. I am not a therapist, but I will listen and I do genuinely care. You listened to me when I needed an ear, so one thing I can give back is my ear. Here is another saying I found. *"When you talk, you are only repeating what you know. But if you listen, you may learn something new."* Sometimes silence is a cry for help, so I need to be more aware of people and their feelings. Not everyone cares about my problems, but if I talk and you listen, I will do the same for you. And not just hear someone spit out words, really listen. Here is another poem I wrote.

Just Shy

I used to think she was just shy,

maybe nervous in front of people.

Or maybe she thought she was too good for any of us.

But I did wonder about her.

She looked nice.

She was pretty in her own way.

Who am I to judge.

I never asked, I didn't think it mattered.

Until the day she took too many pills.

I don't mean to leave on such a sad note, but be aware of those around you.

Day 62

"I can choose to be happy, or choose to be miserable every day waiting until I die." –Angel Haze

Being happy is a choice. It doesn't just happen. The way I was living before, I was miserable. I wasn't living. I was just waiting to die. I was miserable and making everyone around me miserable too. I needed to live, not just exist. I made the choices I did, but had no control of the consequences of those choices. I had to learn from it, and I did. But sometimes the wrong choices bring us to the right places. It's all a crazy circle. But like I've said before everything happens for a reason. I have learned to be happy, and enjoy life. I only live once, so I better make the best of it. God made me, not to be unhappy and live miserably, but to be happy, and feel blessed and live for Him. I have come to the conclusion that my life is the way it is, because he wants me to help others. I want to share my story and hope with others who may feel miserable too. I want to be selfless and go out of my way to help others. I want people to smile when they hear my name, not roll their eyes and shake their heads. So smile today!

Day 63

"No one is going to love you if you don't love yourself."
-unknown

With making myself be happy, with life and with who I am, I have learned that I need to love myself. If I don't love myself, why would anyone else love me? I need to stop hating myself for everything I'm not, and start loving myself for who I am. Learning to love myself is one of the hardest things I have ever done. I have always been self-conscious. I need to worry less about what people think of me. I am who I am, and I'm happy with that. I am learning to be happy with myself. This is how God made me. How can I hate God's creation? Happiness means loving yourself first, so you can share that love with someone else. Each day I want to share my love more, to those around me. I'll end with a poem I wrote.

Inside

I know I am beautiful,
no matter what you say.
I've now learned to be happy
with who I am today.

I've been sad, depressed and lonely,
hurt and full of hate.
But now I see much clearer
Maybe you can relate.

Stop hiding, lying and hurting each other.
We can learn to be real.
Peeling back layers of deep down inside
And show we really feel.

So love yourself today, more than you did yesterday!

Day 64

"Live your life from your heart. Share from your heart.
And your story will touch and heal people's souls."
–Melody Beattie

With my story, I want to share it with others, recovering or not, that there is hope. I hope that me sharing, will help just one person. Help one person to find themselves. To love themselves again. To be open and honest with themselves. To know what is best for them and their family, and THEN DO SOMETHING ABOUT IT!!!

I have told some people some pretty sad, dark things, but that is how I felt at the time, and from that came the "new" me. The title of my first book, "From the Weeds" is based on my life. From the weeds a beautiful flower emerges. With all the crap I have made myself to go through, I have come out on top. So now, the best way to multiply my happiness is to share it with others. Amy Poehler said, *"Continue to share your heart with people even if it's been broken."* I love that. It doesn't matter who you are or what you have done, you are worth it!!! You sharing your story may help someone else. Some people are too ashamed of what they have done, or not done, to think there is any hope, or that they deserve anything better. You are important. You are special. You matter. Know that.

Day 65

"Strive for progress, not perfection" -unknown

I had a friend of mine relapse, and was upset about making the mistake and going back out. Sometimes you fall off the horse, but if you get up and try again, that is progress. If you stay down, you can't blame anyone but yourself. Don't make excuses, make progress. You have that choice to try again. Some may fall off time and time again, but if you get back up and try again, that is progress. Alfred A. Montapert said, "Don't confuse motion with progress. A rocking horse keeps moving, but does not make any progress." If you want it bad enough you will stay on. There are some rocky roads that you will travel, but if you hold on tight, you can make it through anything. You just have to keep your head up and keep looking forward. And if you keep looking back you might fall off too. Look back only to see how far you have come. One day at a time, one step in front of the other. There are always people out there that want to help, but sometimes, we don't see that someone needs help unless their hand is held out. So call out when you need help, before you take that drink. Have someone you can call anytime, and that understands you, and always have a backup. Pick up that 100 lb. phone and reach out.

Day 66

"If I only had three words of advice, they would be, Tell the Truth. If I got three more words. I'd add, all the time." –Randy Pausch

The other day I had someone question me about what I write. I am not here to give advice. This is a journal to myself of how I think I should live, what I think works for me. So if you don't like what I have to say, don't read it. Take what you want, leave what you don't. So here is the only advice I will give. *"Tell the truth!"* I want to state that I am not a therapist, or maybe not the best person to take advice from, (or maybe I should take my own advice) :) But I have learned that the people that give the best advice are usually the ones that have been through the most. So today I will just say to tell the truth, and tell the <u>whole truth</u>, and tell it all the time. I was sick of telling lies, not only to others, but also to myself. I had more lies coming out of my mouth than truth. I was lying to cover up lies that covered up lies. Life is so much easier now, by just being honest. Honest with myself, as well as others.

Day 67

"The love of a family is life's greatest blessing."
-unknown

What a beautiful day to be alive and sober! Yesterday, we celebrated Christmas with my family!!! It was so fun. Some of my cousins I haven't seen in a year. It was so fun to all get together. I'm not going to live in the past, but I remember last Christmas, and I wasn't really "there." I wasn't concerned about anyone but myself. It was all about when I was going to get my next drink. Not that I was making up for lost time this year, but I was. I wanted to enjoy every minute of it. No one is guaranteed life tomorrow, so I want to make and remember as many good memories as I possibly can. It was so fun watching my children play with their cousins, making great memories of their own. We are all so blessed. I am so blessed to have my family. And in sobriety, I have more friends now, that I consider family. I still talk to many friends that made when I was in treatment. We all spent every minute of every day together for weeks, some months. Some of them know more about me, like really "about me" that some of my blood family. I have an extended family now that will always be a part of my life. And for that I am truly grateful.

Day 68

"Sometimes you need to look at life from a different perspective." –Ina Chanboun

Today I look at things in a new light, more of the way they are supposed to be. Before, I was looking at life through the bottom of a bottle. My views were distorted from reality. I was only thinking about me, how everything would affect me, how I only wanted to please myself. I was so selfish. My life was such a mess, but I made it that way. It was finally time to clean house, and enjoy life. I was looking at all the negative, thinking everyone was out to get me. I wasn't looking at all the good around me; an amazing husband, 2 beautiful children, supportive parents, and other friends and family. Once I stopped looking at the world through that bottle, I was seeing it clearly, how blessed I really was. Life is good, I have everything I need. I have a roof over my head, food on the table, and a loving family. I couldn't ask for more. Today I thank God that He gave me that chance to see the way He wanted me to see.

Day 69

"It's crazy to think of some of the stuff we used to care about." -unknown

It is so crazy what I used to care about, what I put first in my life. I was so selfish. I was so worried about making it to the gas station as soon as they opened, so I could be "good" for the day. I was more worried about getting caught, or caught in a lie, regarding my drinking. My priority was a lie. It is pretty pathetic that I had to hide it, to lie about drinking, when everyone knew it. I thought I was hiding it pretty good, when in reality everyone knew there was a real problem. I thought about no one but myself. I had to have alcohol in my system all the time, not because I was having fun anymore. It was so I wouldn't die. I would hide it everywhere, I had to have some vodka somewhere close at all times. Now, I have so much more time to enjoy and not have to lie. There is so much less going on up in my head, because I'm not lying all the time. I don't have to think as much because the truth is so much easier to live. :) I am truly living, and loving life. I enjoy what I care about today, my loves, my life, and laughing. What do you care about?

Day 70

"The best things in life aren't things." –Art Buchwald

Today was a great day! I got to spend the time with my family...sober. I wasn't feeling miserable, impatiently waiting to go home so I could drink, or at least not hide it so much. I was enjoying time with family, laughing and reminiscing. This was such a wonderful day! And the best things about today were not the gifts I received, but the memories we made. Seeing family I hadn't seen in months. I didn't have much to "give." But I gave them me, sober. Today brought back a lot of memories of last Christmas. Now making a fresh new start. The best things I have today, aren't things, they are the love of my family: the laughs, the smiles, the hugs, and stories; fellowship with one another that strengthens our love for one another.

Day 71

"It's not how much we give, but how much we put into giving." –Mother Teresa

I've been thinking a lot lately. (sometimes that's not a good thing) But anyways, about giving…Giving back what I have. And it's not just giving things. It is giving myself. Being vulnerable and showing people the real me. Giving and enjoying it. Not just giving someone something. Like I said yesterday, the things I care about most aren't things; giving myself, sharing, helping others. Not because I want to show people how good I am trying to be, but because I genuinely want to. To be humble. To love what I do when I give; to be willing to go out my way to help someone. Even something small. I get more satisfaction knowing I am not being selfish anymore. The more I give of myself, the better I feel. So help someone today. Give something to someone, not physically, but genuine love.

Day 72

"Our house is clean enough to be healthy, but dirty enough to be happy." -unknown

WOW! After Christmas, I kids got so much, I have no idea where to put it. So this morning, they had a job, to clean up their rooms and toy boxes and get rid of 1 garbage bag full of old toys they don't play with. At first, they were upset and shocked that they would have to do that. BUT this year I explained to them that not all children have toys and we are going to donate them to kids who can't afford them. Then they were excited about sharing their toys. They weren't just getting rid of old worn out toys, they were getting rid of nice, gently used ones too! So far we, between the 2 kids, we have 2 garbage bags full of clothes, and 3 bags of toys. They also feel good about what they are doing! I am so proud of them. I am also going through our home and getting rid of old clothes and stuff I haven't used in 5 years. Our house is messy, but not dirty. It is lived in. That is another thing I am working on in my life, cleaning and organizing. We have a very small house, and have no room for storage, no basement. So, I am keeping what use and getting rid of what we don't. Someday we will have a bigger house, but as for now, we are making do, and cleaning up what we have.

Day 73

"I don't want to be perfect, I want to be honest."
-unknown

I will be the first one to say that for years my life was a lie. My life was one lie after another. Trying to keep everything in my head straight so it went together. Now, I am honest, with others and myself I am not perfect and don't claim to be. And I don't expect anyone else to be either. But it's hard when every day I know someone is living a lie, and can't even be honest with themselves. Who am I to judge, but it so hard when I see someone lying to themselves to make the world around them seem normal. It's hard to see that on a daily basis, they have this greatness radiating from them, but no one knows the truth. I cannot point fingers or diagnose anyone of their issues. I cannot tell someone else's truth either. It is only that person that can do so. I can only look at myself, and keep my side of the street clean. It is hard to do this, but it needs to be done. I can only do me.

Day 74

"The worst lies are the lies we tell ourselves. We live in denial of what we do, even what we think."
-Richard Bach

I was in denial for a long time. I knew I had a problem and wanted help, but I really didn't. I was telling so many lies, I started believing them. I didn't know the truth from the lies. Not only was I lying to others, but to myself. It hurts me to see someone else in denial. I cannot diagnose anyone with anything, but when you see it first hand and know there is a problem and there is nothing you can do about it, it hurts. I was in denial for years, but seeing someone in the exact situation, and they are in denial too, I feel helpless. You can only tell someone so many times how you really feel about what you think of their problem, but until they realize how much of a problem it really is, can anything be done. I am helpless. And I hate that feeling. I want to help someone so bad, but they have to want to help themselves. I am now understanding how they felt about me, but it is even harder knowing the same about them, but they are in denial as well. If they are not willing to make the changes necessary, nothing will change. The misery will continue. I am also now understanding how much my problem affected others, but it hurts even more when someone close to you does the same thing you did to them. So I can only pray.

Day 75

"Nothing makes you more vulnerable than your refusal to be honest with yourself about what you want. –Charly Emery

Being honest and vulnerable is easier said than done. A lot of people hide the truth, because that is easier. They don't want people to judge them. Being honest doesn't hurt, but lying does. It hurts yourself mostly, it can eat you up inside. I would rather be open and honest about myself, troubles and triumphs, than lie about them to look better. The fakeness I had before didn't even make me happy. Another little saying I like is, "Being honest may not get you a lot of friends, but it'll always get you the right ones." One of the first things I had to do in sobriety was to admit that I was powerless over alcohol-that my life had become unmanageable. My life was such a mess, I didn't even know where to begin. But that was the first step. Admitting I had a problem...to myself. That was a personal decision I had to make. No one could make it for me. But now, I am more happy than I have ever been. I don't have that hanging over my head. John 8:32 says, "...the truth will set you free."

Day 76

"Don't look down and be depressed, look up and you will blessed." *-unknown*

In the past, I was too busy looking down and sulking in my self-pity and misery to notice all the good around me. Now, looking up to see what is right in front of my face, I see the love that surrounds me. The love than is undying and true. Just realizing all that I do have, is more rewarding than any material thing. When I looked down all the time, I couldn't see anything. I could only see my feet, and they weren't moving in the right direction. They were trudging slowly, just enough to be moving. Only when I looked up, could I move forward, and go to the place I wanted to be. One day at a time, one foot in front of the other. Looking down I could only see 10% of the world at my feet. Looking up, I go forward, and see around me. I even look back from time to time to see where I was, but not for too long, or it will deter me from my forward movement. Keep your head up and keep moving.

Day 77

"Every new beginning comes from some other beginning's end." –Seneca

Yippee! A new year! A new start! In February of last year, I made a decision to make a change in my life...a big change. This is a new year for a fresh, new start in my life. At the finish line, is just another start line. Life is a continuous circle of beginnings and ends. I have to make sure that what I am ending is to make something better. There are a few ways I could explain last year. It was terrible because I was drinking all the time then had to go to rehab, so last year sucked. But I could also look at it this way. I went to a treatment facility to make my life better, and enjoyed and really "lived" for the rest of the year. So even though it started out bad, it ended up great. I had to hit my bottom to realize that, but I ended up coming out on top. A year ago today, I was feeling miserable, like I did every day. My life was beyond a mess. So today, I thankful to say I made it one more day! One more day sober in the books. Let's start this year off right, and make it better.

Day 78

"This is a new year. A new beginning. And things will change." -unknown

I am so excited to see what this year brings. I started off last year pretty crappy to say the least, but ended up on top. I had to hit my bottom to get where I am today. I started a new chapter in my life 10 months ago, but right now I get the chance to continue that life this year. I love it! It was nice waking up Jan 1st, and not have a hangover. Being sober, I have had more opportunities than I ever have before. I got a new job, and have better relationships with everyone important to me. I know everyone has resolutions and people say most don't last very long, but I have more motivation to do anything than ever before. I have a reason to live now. I have hope. Each day, I pray that God will get me through one more day and keep me sober. Every night I thank Him for his blessings and another day sober. The above quote says that a new year can bring change. I am the one that made that change. It didn't just happen. Yes, I had a lot of love and support, but ultimately I had to work at it to make the change and make it work. Things changed because I changed. I have no control over anything but myself. The only things I do have control over is myself AND how I react to things. So cheers to a new year and a year of positive change.

Day 79

"You can't reach for anything new if your hands are still full of yesterday's junk." –Louise Smith

Starting with a clean slate is a wonderful feeling. But really being able to have a new beginning must mean getting rid of all of yesterday's garbage. I have to get rid of the regret and guilt I feel, to truly feel free. To be released from these chains of shame and anger, I need true peace. It is a decision that must be made, to clean the slate. When you wipe a chalkboard clean, there will still be some chalk dust visible, but only the new writings will be legible. I had to get rid of all the hate and hurt in my heart for the love and peace to replace it. Me being at peace with myself has been a huge part my life's change in recovery.

Day 80

"I have to allow myself to feel the pain of what I am going through if I am to heal." -Sebastian Temlett

Recently, I have been talking about starting over, fresh...changing for the better. But I also don't think that by starting over, you should shove all your feelings of hurt and shame under the rug and leave them there to only grow with time. I needed to feel the feelings that I was hiding before by drinking. They were there for a reason, and needed to be felt, but not all at once or be skewed by my thoughts of reality. I needed to talk to someone, someone I trusted, to get everything off my chest, say how I really felt. I needed to shed all my fears and be open an honest with myself, with how I really felt. Sometimes, I feel that I made myself feel a certain way to make things seem "ok." Lie to myself, about how I really felt. It was easier that way. Feelings are a hard thing to explain. Sometimes it's what your heart tells you to do, and sometimes it's what your heart tells your head to do. It's a hard thing to differentiate. How I feel, or how I think I should feel. But I do notice, if I am looking at all the negative around me, my feelings do get skewed, and I look at how I should feel, not how I really do.

Day 81

"Sometimes the hardest thing and the right thing are the same." -unknown

Sometimes I think I have to deal with the hardest things in life. And ask, "Why?" I have to stop and think that maybe what I am going through now is to get me to a better place. I may not see it now, but God has my life planned out. There is a reason I am put through, or put myself through, everything I am. I think what I want is the best...the way it should be. But a lot of the time I am way off. With relationships, jobs, friendships. Sometimes the hardest thing to do is to let go of what I think is right. But most of the time in hindsight, I see why. It is the hardest thing to understand at the time, why things are going the way they are. Why he broke up with me? Why I lost my job? Why she lied to me? Why? Why? Why? It is difficult to sit back and let God. Let God take the steering wheel and drive this crazy train I'm on. The Lord know, He does a better job than me. :) I have tried far too many times to do things my way or the way I think they should be and it never seems to turn out right. So I just need to patient, and see what God has planned for me. When one door closed, another door opens. I'm never left in the hallway for too long.

Day 82

"Keep your head up. God gives his hardest battles to His strongest soldiers." -unknown

I have a friend going through a hard time right now. I hated when I would be down and depressed and people would say, "Keep your head up." It was true, but so much easier said than done. She is also a little bit of a princess, so I found another quote for her. *"Keep your head up, princess. Your tiara is falling."* :) But so much of what people say, quotes and advice, so much easier to spit the words out than to live by them. And it does take time to get through things. Some people say to get over it. But a lot of the time, you need to get through it, not over it. It's not just something you can forget about. It may be something very important to you, someone. You obviously can't just forget that person ever existed, but remember both the good and bad. There is a reason it isn't the way it used to be. For me, my addiction to alcohol was a relationship in and of itself. It was a priority to me. When I quit, I broke up with it; it was a hard to get over. But with all time, time heals, or at least helps. I wouldn't say it ever "heals." There will always be a scar, a reminder of what was there, but it does get better, and easier. So keep your head up, buttercup!

Day 83

"Sometimes when things are falling apart, they may actually be falling into place."

I've been thinking a lot about how I used to think. I used to think that my way was the best way. Looking back now, all the crazy things I thought should or shouldn't have happened or "Why did I do that?" I see now. There are things today still that I question if are paths I should take. But if I just look to God and let Him take control, my life is less stressful. In my life I thought that with my drinking and using, no one would ever look at me the same, as if I was tainted. But now I can see that what I did and went through may be able to help someone else! My goal today is to help others, give back what I have learned and live it every day. Not just speak it, live it. I've said it a million times, and you've heard it too, everything happens for a reason. Billy Wilder said, "Hindsight is always 20/20."; the future, not so much. So when you think things are falling apart, they may really be falling in to place.

Day 84

"In three words I can sum up everything about life: it goes on." –Robert Frost

We all have ups and downs in our lives. Good times and bad; triumphs and struggles, but there is one thing true...life goes on. It doesn't stop when it's bad, and it doesn't stop when it's great. It is continually moving. But sometimes it seems we are never happy where we are at this moment. We are anxiously waiting for the next good thing, or wishing the past would be farther removed. I have learned to live in the moment. Each one is given to us to enjoy, to remember, to cherish. We have all been through hard times, either financial, emotional, deaths of loved ones and friends, job loss, something. But we have also all been through some great things. We need to be grateful for all that we do have. Remember the bad times, so you can appreciate the good ones more.

Day 85

"If it scares you, it might be a good thing to try." –Seth
Godin

I am going to start off by saying today's quote is not true for <u>everything</u>. So don't take it literally and try everything that scares you. You don't have to jump out of a plane, or walk a tight rope. But I'm talking about change. Getting sober scared me; it was a change. Getting a new job scared me; it was a change. Making new friends scared me, it was a change. But when I was the way I was, "comfortable," my life was falling apart. I had to change for anything to get better, and all that scared me. Making these decisions scared the heck out of me, but when I gave it to God, He took away the fear. Putting it in His hands, took the weight off me. I knew I wasn't alone. So for me, trying the thing that scared me most, was the best thing I ever did!!!

Day 86

"Another day; another blessing!"

Today I have been sober for 11 months. One day at a time. Only by the grace of God have I been able to stay sober...one day at a time. Every day is a blessing. A day to be grateful for all the things God has given me. All the things He has let me experience, feel, and enjoy. There is not ONE day that I wish I would have stayed where I was...in that dark hole I had dug for myself. Not one day I wish I wouldn't have stopped drinking. Not one day I regret making the biggest, hardest choice in my life. Every day I feel so blessed to be given this opportunity to share my story with others. To not be embarrassed and ashamed of my past, but to join with others in recovery and rise above this hell we created and wallowed in for who knows how long. Today I am blessed to be alive, clean, and sober one more day!

Day 87

"A true friend is someone who thinks that you are a good egg, even though he knows that you are slightly cracked." –Bernard Meltzer

I deeply appreciate the friends that I do have. It's nice to know that they don't judge me. I've come to the point where I am not worried about what people think of me. I know who I am, who God made me to be. I really have learned who my real friends are. Who really cares for me as a person, as I do them. I have also learned not to judge as I did before either. I was worried about people judging me while I was doing the same thing. It's hard to live as a hypocrite, saying one thing and doing another. Looking down a someone for doing one thing, when I was doing the exact same thing! This has really become a self-seeking opportunity. For me to find myself, who I am, who I want to be. I want to be the friend someone is proud to have, proud to share life's experiences with. I want to love, and care for, and be true to. I want to be the best friend I can be.

Day 88

"Being honest may not get you a lot of friends but it'll always get you the right ones." –John Lennon

In sobriety, I have learned to be more honest, with others and myself. By doing this, I may not get a lot of friends, but I will get the good ones. Good friends are hard to find. But if I just be myself, and true to myself, I will find the rights ones, and they will be there forever. Being a good friend, is not just sharing a cup of coffee, or funny story, but also really sharing your heart and soul. Not just being friends on the outside, for others to see, but really be there for each other. To be able to trust each other with everything, telling each other what makes them hurt, or what makes them happy. Don't try to be perfect, be honest.

Day 89

"There is no path to happiness. Happiness is the path."

I have learned to be happy and it does not have a finish line. It is a path. Dr Steve. Maraboli said, *"Happiness is a state of mind, a choice, a way of living; it is not something to be achieved, it is something to be experienced."* It is not something made, but a result of my actions. I used to think, "Oh, I just want to be happy...or...if such and such would happen I would be happy"...so on and so on. It was something I was chasing, something I was trying to attain. I thought there was something I had to do to get it. I have learned that I have to make that choice to be happy. God has given me so many things to be grateful for, and happy about. I am so blessed. Out of the 100 good things that happen, I used to look at the 5 bad things, and focus on them. I would let that rule my life. I wouldn't remember the 95 good things, that more than outweighed the bad. So today I choose to be happy.

Day 90

"Unity is strength… when there is teamwork and collaboration, wonderful things can be achieved."
–Mattie J.T. Stepanek

Today I am going to talk about unity. When I was drinking, it was all about me, me, me. I thought of no one but myself. Getting sober was a very humbling experience. I learned I cannot do things on my own. Associating with other recovering alcoholic/addicts, I see that we can help each other one day at a time to stay sober. If I didn't have fellowship, I would lose myself, and my strength. I know I cannot do it on my own, and need to stay with them. When we work together and express our ideas and experiences of strength and hope, it is so much easier. That also goes for every aspect of my life. Working as a team with my husband, to raise our children. Working together at work, being part of the team. Getting involved in whatever I do, not just sit on the sidelines and watch. Get in there and get busy.

Day 91

"The most important thing in communication is to hear what isn't being said." –Peter Drucker

At work yesterday, I was listening to a book on tape called, "Crucial conversations." WOW! What a wake up call. I heard things I never thought of or if I did, knew that was how I was supposed to talk to people, but it never came out like that. In my head, I am always right. In reality, I'm not and it's hard to for me to accept that. My defense mechanism is sarcasm. I would use it with my husband all the time!!! I think things in my head, and think he is supposed to know exactly how I feel, when he might be totally clueless. The way I look at things may be totally opposite from the way he thinks, but I think he should feel the same way I do. We grew up in two totally different lifestyles at home. But we need to respect the way each other feels and compromise and least listen. Too much of the time, what I *say* may not be what I *mean.* What I hear myself say what I think I said it comes out degrading. I don't mean to sound mean, but it may come out that way. I need to work on patience and listening not just hearing, and valuing his opinion, and respect how he feels. I need to be aware of his feelings, and genuinely care. And when I'm wrong, suck it up, and apologize. Not just say I'm sorry, but apologize with a sincere change of heart. That's all I have for now.

Day 92

"The single biggest problem in communication is the illusion that it has taken place." George Bernard Shaw

More today about communication. I really like this quote. So much of the time I think what I am trying to get across is what they are hearing from me. The thought of good communication, when in fact is, it is way off, is worse than none at all. John Powell said, *"Communication works for those who work at it."* If you don't try, it won't ever happen. It is something you have to work on. I have always thought I had good communication skills, but the more I really look at it, I am good at expressing how I feel and being honest about it now. But me listening and really hearing what you say, is the whole other side of communication. It is a two way street. I need to express to you how I feel, but also need to listen to your voice. Work as a team to really understand each other and respect each other. I have always been outgoing and outspoken. But am learning to be more modest and quiet. I am trying to be more of a listener. I still talk a lot. LOL. But am trying to slow down and listen more. Practicing daily, true communication and conversations.

Day 93

"No relationship can survive without trust, honesty, and communication, no matter how close you are."
-J. Sterling

Listening and communication have been a topic the past few days. A relationship is based on trust. Without trust, there is nothing. To be able to trust, you have to be honest, and to be fully honest there must be an open line of communication. All these things together create a relationship. A relationship is based on these three principles with the triangle holding it together. Without one of them, the relationship has a faulty foundation. Poor bad communication can cause honesty issues which in turn shakes the trust factor. Each one needs the other. They are all dependent on the others. Each day I face these facts. In any relationship I have, be it family, friends, or even work. I realized that when I got out of treatment, I was going to have to <u>earn</u> people's trust back. It was NOT go to be easy. They weren't just going to give it to me. But for me to do that, I had to work on the other 2 factors, to improve my chances at ever getting that back. I have to be honest, and open, and communicate to those my feelings. I have heard another phrase, *"Trust is like a piece of paper, once it is crumpled it will never be perfect."* I know this, but can only do what I can with what I have, and that will have to do. I crumpled up that paper, now I am ironing out. Day by day, it is getting smoother.

Day 94

"Don't trust words, trust actions.

When I was in treatment, I knew I was going to have to earn my trust back from everyone: my husband, my children, my parents, friends, and boss. Each one was going to be different. I lied to all of them, but in different ways. I lied to make myself think that what I was doing, ok. I had broken each person's trust in different way. I knew that just me saying I was sorry, was not going to be enough. You can only say sorry so many times, before it has no meaning at all. All too soon, it just becomes words you say, to make yourself feel better after doing something wrong. Saying sorry is different than apologizing. To me, an apology is a true change of heart, an understanding that I was wrong, in what I did or said. And my trust was not going to be gained my telling everyone I was sorry, and I wasn't ever going to do it again. It was earned by actions. By living what I was sorry for, in the right way day after day. I had to be able to trust myself too. Another phrase I like is, *"Trust takes years to earn, seconds to break, and forever to repair."* Boy is that true. I know for some people, I may never fully get their trust back, and that is my own fault. But I can work every day towards that; to be honest, and truthful; to be living my words through actions.

Day 95

"Coming together is the beginning. Keeping together is progress. Working together is success." –Henry Ford

Getting sober has made be less selfish. I am in no way saying I am perfect now, just getting better at my flaws. Knowing I can't do things alone. I have stopped trying to do everything myself. What Henry Ford said, can be used in all aspects of my life; family and business. It is not just coming together, but staying and working at it. A relationship needs these to work. Working together is the key. It is a process. It doesn't just magically happen. You have to work at it, together, both parties. In personal relationships this is not just physical, but an emotional and spiritual job. My husband and I have had to work through a lot during the past few years. We arc at an understanding of each other's needs and respect each other's opinions and compromise to make it work. We have become a team instead of two individuals working toward the same goal, but each doing it our own way. Teamwork is an important piece of success. It's amazing what we can accomplish when we work together.

Day 96

"The love between a mother and daughter is forever."

Today is my daughter's 7th birthday. I am so proud of her. She is an amazing, smart, funny girl. This past year, our relationship has grown so much. For a while I was just a mom, that took care of her physical needs, and attempted to be there, but with alcohol involved, it wasn't 100%. I will never be able to get back that time, but I can only do what I can today, and that is to be the best mom I can be. The mom my kids deserve to have. She has always loved me, but I feel now we are closer, have a stronger bond than before. She was at the age where I thought she didn't know what was going on, but she did. She is smart and sees me as the mom that will always be there for me. The mom she can tell anything to. The mom she can trust to help her through anything. (and the Lord knows, I have probably done it.)

On the other hand, with my mom too; for a while, I pushed her away. I wanted to do things my way, the right way. (right) ₊) But I finally figured out, I couldn't do it alone. She has always been there for me, to love me, to care for me, to listen to me, to forgive me. Today I am trying to be the best mom and daughter I can be. I love you mom! I love you Laney and happy birthday! Love you, love you, love you!

Day 97

"I don't forgive people because I'm weak. I forgive them because I'm strong enough to know people make mistakes."

I am thinking a lot about forgiveness. I have learned I need to forgive others as fast as I think God should forgive me. I also shouldn't do "bad" things only because I know God will forgive me. I have to really think whom else it will hurt, and how they may forgive me. Is what I'm doing really worth, hurting others. What am I getting out of it? People make mistakes. Lord knows I've done my share, and still will. Just hopefully, not like I was making. Not making the same mistakes, over and over and over again. It was a vicious circle of messing up, saying I was sorry, making broken promises, and doing it again. It was insanity. Today I know we all make mistakes and I can't hold grudges forever for people doing wrong things. That is hypocritical. I have been there, and expected forgiveness, now I should do the same. Today I don't forgive because I have to, but because I want to. I truly understand the imperfect nature of humans. I am stronger today for making mistakes and learning from them, not staying in that selfish circle of lies.

Day 98

"If you can't figure out your purpose, figure out your passion. For your passion will lead you right into your purpose."

I had previously walked through life feeling as if I had no purpose. Well, I guess I was here to be a wife and mother, but that was about it. I really didn't feel like I was here to do anything. Once I got sober, I had a whole new outlook. I was here for a reason. I had a purpose. Maybe it was to go through part of my life as an alcoholic/addict, to be able to help others recovering as well. I feel that what I have done helps me communicate better to those who want the same thing I have, the same thing I want, sobriety. My passion now is life: loving it and living it. Loving what I have and understanding how truly blessed I am, is an amazing thing. God didn't give me a second chance it was all part of His plan. If I wasn't an alcoholic, I wouldn't be able to help other alcoholics. I wouldn't be able to appreciate what I do have. Who knows what I would be doing. But not doing what I love: helping people, caring for people, sharing with people, loving people. Do what you love and you will love what you do. I am so happy now, so full of joy, and THAT is an amazing thing.

Day 99

"Live your life from your heart. Share from your heart.
And your story will touch and heal people's souls."
–Melody Beattie

I am now actually living. Before, I was going through the motions, and watching life pass me by. I have learned to life like there is no tomorrow. I want to genuinely share my life's journey. I keep saying "to other alcoholic/addicts", but in reality I should be saying everyone. I don't need to separate myself from others. Those not struggling with addiction or alcoholism may get something out of what I say too. What I say doesn't only deal with alcoholic/addicts, it can be used in daily life. Also, what I say, it just my opinion, not what I think you should do, or how you should live. It is just how I feel about where I was, compared to where I am today. I notice a huge difference in myself, in my attitude on everything, work and family life. I feel more like an asset to my family, than a hindrance. Before, with my depression and hatefulness toward everything, I resonated a negative aura. With my current, positive, attitude, I feel so blessed. God has given me so much to live for, and just realizing that was a huge step. So hopefully me sharing the hope we have in God, will help just one person, get through one more day. I probably won't change the world, but me sharing in this book, if anyone reads it or not, is healing to me.

Day 100

"Take care of your body. It's the only place you have to live." –Jim Rohn

For my New Year's resolution, I chose to be healthier, like a million other people. But I am serious. Last year started off terrible. I got into a bad car accident, and then went to rehab, but that's what started my sobriety. After treatment, I learned that I had to take care of myself. At that point I was more focused on the mental side. I was such a mess from drinking, I didn't know which way was up. In treatment, they said it would be months, maybe a year before my head would be clear. When I was 30 days sober, I thought I knew everything and was thinking right again. But as the months passed it got clearer and clearer. It's crazy. Looking back now, I was nowhere near clearheaded, but it sure was a lot more than clear than when I was using. Today, at almost 1 year sober, I have never felt this good in my life. Since I have been so focused on my mental state and consciousness, I have been slacking a little on my physical state. Before, I was drinking all the time, and I never ate. I was drinking empty calories. I was thinner, but had a very distended abdomen from the swelling of my insides. Once I got sober, I had to learn to eat again; to eat healthy. At first, it was hard, I wasn't used to eating food, nonetheless healthy food. In treatment, we had 3 meals per day, with healthy snacks in between. When I got home, I had to make food. (something I had never really done before) Now I cook regularly. Needless to say, I put on a few pounds. So as of January 1st, I started working out every day, and eating healthier. I have learned that food that is good for you doesn't have to be food that doesn't taste good. So now, it is time to take care of the physical me. It was hard at first, but so was getting sober. So I use the same mindset for this. Once day at a time. I don't have to tell myself I am going to work out for the rest of my life...one day at a time. It actually feels good now to be sore. It feels like I am doing something. I am proud of myself, for what I have done in my life. Where I am today; who I have become.

There are 100 of my days sober. To read more, go to my daily updated blog at laurenyoder.weebly.com where I continue to journal my sober journey. One day at a time!

I enjoy sharing my experience, strength and hope with others. Who knows, maybe someday I will publish 100 more...

12376484R00095

Printed in Great Britain
by Amazon.co.uk, Ltd.,
Marston Gate.